UNCONDITIONAL LOVE OF
YOUR HEAVENLY FATHER

cherished

©2021 Lifeway Press®

ISBN 978-1-0877-4425-4
Item 005831814
Dewey Decimal Classification Number: 242
Subject Heading: DEVOTIONAL LITERATURE / BIBLE STUDY AND TEACHING / GOD

Printed in the United States of America

Student Ministry Publishing
LifeWay Resources
One LifeWay Plaza
Nashville, Tennessee 37234

publishing team

Director, Student Ministry
Ben Trueblood

Manager, Student Ministry Publishing
John Paul Basham

Editorial Team Leader
Karen Daniel

Writer
Mary Margaret West

Content Editor
Stephanie Cross

Production Editor
Brooke Hill

Graphic Designer
Kaitlin Redmond

We believe that the Bible has God for its author; salvation for its end; and truth, without any mixture of error, for its matter and that all Scripture is totally true and trustworthy. To review LifeWay's doctrinal guideline, please visit www.lifeway.com/doctrinalguideline.

table of contents

intro

We all want to be loved for who we are wherever we are right now. We want to be lovable in this very moment—no matter our joys or sorrows, victories or mistakes, beauties or flaws. Girls especially were designed with a deep desire for being loved in spite of our imperfections. Put simply: We want to be cherished.

Being cherished means we are protected, cared for, held dear, treated with tenderness, and deeply loved. This is exactly how God loves us. Scripture shows us this truth over and over again.

- He protects us eternally—no one and nothing can separate us from Him (John 10:28-30; Rom. 8:37-39).

- Jesus "provides and cares for," or cherishes, the church (Eph. 5:29).

- We are God's children, "holy and dearly loved" (Col. 3:12).

- God carries us close and leads us gently (Isa. 40:11).

- God loves us so deeply that He sent His own Son, Jesus, to die for us—even as we were still sinners (Rom. 5:8).

Those passages contain only a few of the endless examples of God's absolute love for us. His love is full and fulfilling; it is a "come as you are" love. His love brings us to the highest mountains to rejoice and drives us to our knees in gratitude and humility. His love is holy, sweet, gentle, and overwhelming in the best way. And His love—the way He cherishes us—is completely, 100 percent unconditional. The biblical term for this is *agape*.

Here's the good news: God loves you right where you are. No matter what you've done or how many times you've thought, "He wouldn't love me, not after what I've done"—God loves you. This is the greatest gift we've ever been given, and over the next 30 days, we'll examine what God's *agape* love means for us.

getting started

This devotional contains 30 days of content, broken down into sections that answer a specific question about God's *agape* love. Each day is divided into three elements—discover, delight, and display—to help you answer core questions related to Scripture.

discover

This section helps you examine the passage in light of who God is and determine what it says about your identity in relationship to Him. Included here is the daily Scripture reading, focus passage, along with illustrations and commentary to guide you as you study.

delight

In this section, you'll be challenged by questions and activities that help you see how God is alive and active in every detail of His Word and your life.

display

Here's where you take action. Display calls you to apply what you've learned through each day's study.

prayer

Each day also includes a prayer activity in one of the three main sections.

Throughout the devotional, you'll also find extra articles and activities to help you connect with the topic personally, such as such as Scripture memory verses, additional resources, and questions.

day 1

WHAT IS LOVE?

discover |

READ 1 CORINTHIANS 13.

It bears all things, believes all things, hopes all things, endures all things.
—1 Corinthians 13:7

The English language doesn't do the word *love* justice. We use the same word when saying, "I love tacos" and "I love my parents." But that doesn't make sense, does it? Just like our English language limits us with describing love, we are also limited in our understanding of the word *love* when it comes to how God loves us. We sing about it, we talk about it, and we hope for it, but we don't have a great understanding of what love truly is until we look at God. His love is bigger than we can imagine and can weather any storm.

We'll spend this month digging into the word *agape*—God's unconditional, sacrificial love for us. It's hard for us to wrap our brains around the idea of someone loving us unconditionally—no matter what. We're used to people walking away when we've upset them or rejecting the love that we're offering, but God's love is different. It can withstand anything (1 Cor. 13:7). There's nothing that can separate us from God's love, and He's in it for the long haul with us (Rom. 8:38-39).

Before you move forward, spend a few minutes asking God to help you see His *agape* love for you. Think back to today's key verse, and praise God that His love for us, "bears all things, believes all things, hopes all things, and endures all things." Tell Him how much you love Him and how you want to understand His love in a fresh, new way. If you haven't shown love to those around you lately, pray that God would give you an opportunity to share His love wherever you go.

delight |

What's your response when you love someone but don't receive love from them in return?

Thinking back on the last week, what's one way you can see God's love for you in your life?

How does knowing that God loves you unconditionally change the way you think about Him? Explain.

display |

If you want to grow in your love toward others, the best way is to understand God's love for you. As we walk through this month, ask a godly older woman in your life to share a story of how she has seen God show His love for her. One of the best ways to learn is through stories, so don't miss the chance to hear her story and let it increase your faith and love for God. Consider letting her be a mentor to you as you walk through this devotional and grow in your love for God.

day 2

HARD TO LOVE

discover

READ 1 JOHN 4:7-21.

And we have this command from him: The one who loves God must also love his brother and sister. —1 John 4:21

God loves you. Did you know that? He really loves you! He loves you right where you are, no matter what your life has looked like up until this exact moment. He loves you in spite of mistakes, heartaches, and flaws. God sees you exactly as you are and He loves you. Because of the love He shows to us, we're able to show love to those around us. He loves you because He is love.

In an interesting turn of events, John wrote, "The one who loves God must also love his brother and sister." Yikes. We love being loved, but that means we have to love everyone? In this case, brother and sister aren't just siblings, but the people God has placed in your life. Yes, even the ones who don't seem very lovable. Let's be real—some people are hard to love. God says that loving others isn't optional; it's how we're supposed to live our lives if we say we love Him. The more you love others, the more you'll be able to fully experience the love of God.

When you begin to love others the way that you've been loved, it's a total game changer. You'll become less selfish, you'll be on the lookout for ways to serve the people God has placed in your life, and you'll better understand the depth of God's love for you.

delight |

What is your typical response when you don't feel loved by others?

How does knowing that loving others isn't optional change your perspective?

Before you wrap up today, answer the question, "Do I know how much God loves me?" Maybe you need to re-read today's verses and see how God shows love toward His people.

display |

Understanding God's love for you is key to understanding how to love others. Let your actions lead the way, even if it takes a little while for your feelings to catch up. Like you read earlier, the more you love others, the more you'll be able to fully experience the love of God.

Who are some girls in your life that you have a tough time loving? Think of one way you can love at least one of those girls this week.

Now that you've thought of a few people that are hard to love, spend some time praying specifically for them. You'll be surprised at how prayer can change your perspective toward someone. Ask God to help you in this important area of obedience. If you don't feel very loved by God today, ask Him to show you how loved you are. Ask God to change your heart and your perspective, especially when it comes to loving people who are hard to love.

day 3

IT ALL COMES DOWN TO JESUS

---

discover |

READ JOHN 3:11-21.

For God loved the world in this way: He gave his one and only Son, so that everyone who believes in him will not perish but have eternal life. For God did not send his Son into the world to condemn the world, but to save the world through him. —John 3:16–17

These are some of the most powerful verses found in the Bible. They tell the story of the gospel in such a clear and simple way. You've probably heard these verses before, or at least verse 16. There's no greater example of sacrifice in the Bible or all of history than God sending His Son to earth, all the while knowing that Jesus' death would be the only way to accomplish God's salvation plan for us.

The world is in your backyard. There are people in your neighborhood, your school, or your team who don't have a relationship with Jesus. Here's the deal—all of those girls you thought of yesterday that are hard to love? Jesus died for them, too. He came so that "everyone who believes in him will not perish but have eternal life." It's easy for your world to become small when all you think about are the things right in front of you—family, school, sports, activities, church, social media. Don't miss the opportunity to tell people in your world about Jesus.

Pray that God would give you eyes to see the people in your world in a new, fresh way. Ask Him to give you an opportunity to share your story with them and for them to be open and receptive to hearing about Jesus. Discouragement can easily distract us, so pray against any discouragement that could keep you from sharing the gospel.

delight |

Have you ever had the opportunity to share your faith in Jesus with someone in your life? If you have, write about it!

Are there girls in your world that you know don't know Jesus? Write their names below and pray specifically for them today.

display |

It might be hard to tell someone else about your relationship with Jesus if you've never thought much about it before. Take some time and write out your faith journey—where you grew up, if you've been involved with church, when you placed your faith in Jesus, and any other event or important moment in your life. Talk about it with your youth pastor, small group leader, or another godly adult in your life, and practice sharing your story with them.

Choose one of the girls you know doesn't know Jesus and commit to sharing the gospel with her this month.

day 4

THIS WILL HURT ME MORE...

discover|

READ HEBREWS 12:3-13.

My son, do not take the Lord's discipline lightly or lose heart when you are reproved by him, for the Lord disciplines the one he loves and punishes every son he receives. —Hebrews 12:6

Discipline is hard. We don't like getting in trouble, and we don't like the consequences that come after it's all over. But Scripture makes it clear that part of the way God shows His love for us is that He disciplines us. The fact of the matter is that sin has consequences, and when we sin, it breaks God's heart.

Have your parents ever told you that discipline is harder on them than it is on you? At the moment, it sounds ridiculous, but it's really true. It's often more difficult to discipline someone than to receive the discipline itself. When Scripture says, "for the Lord disciplines the one he loves," it's a reminder that God doesn't love disciplining us, but He does it so we can learn from our mistakes and grow in our relationship with Him.

One of the hardest parts about discipline is dealing with the consequences. Maybe you've had your phone taken away, couldn't participate in an activity, or lost some privileges. It's hard, but your parents have a point. We don't always understand God's consequences in the moment, but they're meant to be learning experiences. You have to decide if you'll view it that way. Once you lean into the tough situation and begin to learn, you'll recognize that it's for your good and for God's glory. As you deal well with discipline, don't miss the opportunity to point it all back to God.

delight |

How do you typically react when you face discipline?

If discipline sounds harsh to you, how does it change your perspective to know that it comes from a place of love?

How has God used consequences in a positive way in your life?

> Pray that you would be open to discipline and consequences next time they come around in your life. Pray that you would be able to learn from past mistakes so you're not facing the same discipline over and over again. Ask God to help you to make wise choices so you're not faced with consequences in the future.

display |

If you've ever had a pet (especially a dog), you've probably had to show loving discipline at some point. Maybe they dumped over the trash can, had an accident in your bedroom, or chewed up your favorite pair of shoes. It's hard to not get mad, but discipline is key to teaching them what to do differently next time. You lovingly remind them, put them in time out, or redirect their attention to something else, but you don't throw them out on the curb. Grab a squishy toy or small stick—anything that reminds you of a dog—and place it in your backpack, purse, car, or anywhere you'll see it to remind you of the way God lovingly disciplines.

In a journal, write out the words *From my mistakes and consequences, I choose to grow.* Then, journal about a time when you faced consequences for your actions and chose to view them as a learning experience.

day 5

discover |

READ 1 JOHN 4:18.

There is no fear in love; instead, perfect love drives out fear, because fear involves punishment. So the one who fears is not complete in love.

Yesterday you read about how God disciplines those He loves. When it comes to your relationship with God, discipline shouldn't ever lead you to fear. God isn't out to get you, and He's not punishing you "just because." He disciplines you out of love because He values you so much. God's Word tells us, "There is no fear in love; instead, perfect love drives out fear." This should help you understand God's character in a new way.

You should never live in fear of God, but always respect and revere Him as the creator and keeper that He is. We're not supposed to be scared of or intimidated by Him. These are two totally different kinds of fear, and it's really important to understand the difference between the two. Having a healthy fear of God means you always put Him in the right place in your life. He comes near to us, but He's still God. His love for us draws us to Himself, and because of this, we can have a relationship with Him.

Can you imagine being close to someone, but always living in fear of them? That's not at all how God wants us to relate to Him. Think about it this way—most likely, you've had a teacher who is firm, but kind. They don't allow craziness in their classroom, and they ask for respect. Because they are firm and do what they say they're going to do, you give them your respect. This is how God is, but an even better, perfect version!

delight |

What's your typical response to not feeling loved?

Have you ever seen God as someone to be feared? How does the truth that there's no fear in love change the way you view God? Explain.

display |

Hopefully you have a new or fresh view of how God sees you after today's devotion. Listen to a worship song that talks about who God is. Let the words of that song remind you of His character and His desire to love you and know you. Create a playlist of songs that like this that remind you of who God is in your life.

Maybe a relationship in your life has brought you fear, and that has affected the way you view and trust God. If you've ever struggled with this, tell God about it. Ask Him to help you know He can be trusted. If you haven't struggled with this kind of fear, praise God that He has shown you through others that He is worthy of your trust.

day 6

NOTHING. NADA. ZILCH. ZERO.

discover

READ ROMANS 8:31-39.

For I am persuaded that neither death nor life, nor angels nor rulers, nor things present nor things to come, nor powers, nor height nor depth, nor any other created thing will be able to separate us from the love of God that is in Christ Jesus our Lord. —Romans 8:38-39

Romans 8 tells us that there's nothing that can separate us from God's love. Isn't that incredible? It's easy to think that we have to earn God's love, and if we don't do our part, then He won't love us anymore. That simply isn't true. He loves us right where we are, just as we are. The big thing to remember is that He doesn't want us to stay that way. As you grow in your relationship with Jesus, the goal is that you would become more like Him in every area of your life.

When you become a Christian, you are in Christ. That means you are part of Him, and nothing can change it. God is so serious about this that He also says, "things present nor things to come," which means that nothing you've done or ever will do can separate you from Jesus. You can't run far enough from Him, and there's nothing that can pull hard enough to pull you away.

Does this mean that we can do whatever we want now? No! It means that we should live in a thankful way, honoring God with our words, actions, and our very lives. We are called to be grateful and humble, and always point the glory back to God. This isn't a "get out of jail free" card for us, but something that should drive us to live in a way that reflects what Jesus has done for us.

If you're a Christian, praise God that nothing can separate you from Him. That's a big deal! Thank Him that He has given you that security and promise.

If you don't yet have a relationship with Jesus, pray that He would become real in your life. Pray for understanding of what you're reading from the Bible and these devotions, and ask God for wisdom in this chapter of your life.

delight |

How does it make you feel to know that nothing can separate you from Jesus?

Now that you know this, what does it cause you to think about differently? Is there anything in your life that needs to change?

display |

Maybe you haven't been living in a way that shows God you're grateful for what He's done for you through Jesus. It could be that you've been living like you have a free pass. Even if that isn't the case for you, think of how your life should be different because of what you've learned about His love. Today, don't miss the opportunity to fully live your life, celebrating that you belong in Christ. Write the word *Nothing* on an index card or sticky note. Place it on your bathroom mirror to remind you of what can separate you from His love. Make this index card or sticky note as creative as you like—maybe try some hand lettering or drawing pictures that represent the way this idea affects you.

day 7

PROOF

discover |

READ ROMANS 5:6-11.

But God proves his own love for us in that while we were still sinners, Christ died for us. —Romans 5:8

Even with all of your sin, your mistakes, and your mess, Jesus died for you. For *you*. God isn't surprised by your sin, but it disappoints Him and breaks His heart. The main way God showed us His *agape* love was by sending Jesus to die on the cross for our sins. Jesus was the ultimate sacrifice. His blood shed on the cross made a way for us to have a relationship with God and spend eternity in heaven with Him. It is a huge deal that God was willing to sacrifice His own Son for each of us.

God tells us throughout Scripture that He loves us, but Romans 5:8 shows us when it says, "God proves his own love for us in that while we were still sinners, Christ died for us." He gave us a physical, real, living demonstration of the depth of His love for each of us. It wasn't easy, but it was the only way. God didn't just say how much He loved us, He showed us.

delight |

What's something you can do today to show God how much you love Him in response to what He has done for you?

When you think about your own sin, how does it make you feel to know that God is aware of all of it?

How does it change things to know that when you ask Him for forgiveness, God forgets your sin?

display |

On the same card where you wrote the word *Nothing* yesterday, write *Jesus died for* _____ (write your name in the blank). Put the card back on your bathroom mirror or somewhere else you can see it every day. We all need a reminder sometimes, and it can be helpful to see this first thing in the morning or right before you go to bed. Maybe take a picture of it on your phone or save it as your lock screen. Whenever you feel discouraged or frustrated, remind yourself that Jesus died for you. Like we talked about yesterday, nothing can separate you from His love.

Think of a girl you have a tough time loving. Write out *Jesus died for* _____ (her name in the blank). Keep this card with you as a reminder to pray for and share the gospel with this girl.

> Spend a few minutes in prayer. Ask God to help you understand the depths of His love for you. Thank Him that He sent Jesus to die for your sins, and confess that you need Him to remind you of His love for you.

But God proves his own love for us in that while we were still sinners, Christ died for us.

ROMANS 5:8

Tip: As you memorize this Scripture, try writing each word on an index card. Don't forget to include the reference! Place all the cards in order, and say the verse aloud to yourself. Repeat this process, removing one card each time, challenging yourself to fill in the missing word. Do this until there are no words left, and you have memorized the verse.

day 8

GOD'S BIG PLAN

discover

READ GENESIS 3:8-15.

I will put hostility between you and the woman, and between your offspring and her offspring. He will strike your head, and you will strike his heel.
—Genesis 3:15

God has always had a plan. His love for us started at the very beginning and is still in motion today. The Book of Genesis starts off with the creation of the world, the sky, the seas, the night and day, and the animals and creatures of the earth. God created a place for us to live and thrive, and it was all good in His eyes. He then created man in His image (Adam), and created a wife for him (Eve). God's plan was very good from the very beginning.

Was God surprised when sin entered the world? Nope. He was disappointed, but He had a plan. It would be easy to think that God had to think of what to do next, but He didn't. Once Adam and Eve realized they had sinned, they hid from God. Adam tried to shift the blame to her, and then Eve put the blame on the serpent. It was a mess!

Because of sin, God gave Adam and Eve consequences. The serpent—the ultimate deceiver—had influenced their decisions. Today's verse included God's first promise of a Savior and that the serpent would one day be crushed. It is only because of the grace of God that Adam and Eve didn't die that day. Their sin deserved death, but God, who is full of grace and love, spared their lives and promised a Savior would come. Satan would bruise the heel of Jesus, but Jesus would one day crush his head.

Pray that you would see evidence of God's love and grace in your life today.

delight |

What are some of the effects of sin you can see in your everyday world?

What comes to mind when you think about the fact that God has always had a plan—including a plan for you?

How have you seen evidence of God's grace and love in your life?

How does God's promise of a Savior and grace for our sin make you feel cherished?

display |

Does your life reflect the love and grace that God extends toward you? Rather than being quick with your words, pray that God would give you patience and eyes to see the girls in your life the way that He sees them. Where you would normally act or speak quickly, ask God for wisdom as you respond, so that the love of Christ shows through your words and actions.

As you go about your day today, name one way you can extend grace and love to a girl who needs it.

day 9

LAST MAN STANDING

discover |

READ GENESIS 6:5-22.

"But I will establish my covenant with you, and you will enter the ark with your sons, your wife, and your sons' wives." —Genesis 6:18

Noah must have been doing something right. Out of all the people in the world, he was the only man God shared His plan with. Genesis 6 tells us that Noah was righteous and blameless, and most importantly—he walked with God.

Noah did everything God told him to do. Everything. His trust in God was unmatched, and he was faithful to do exactly what God asked of him. The covenant God made with Noah is incredibly important to our understanding God. His covenants were godly promises, and they were very different from a contract because they weren't made to be broken. God promised protection over Noah's family and that He would never destroy the earth by flood again. The rainbow you often see in the sky after a rainstorm is the sign of God's covenant promise to Noah and to us.

Because of Noah's faithfulness, God spared him and his family. God's love extended toward them and all of the creatures He created. All the people on earth except for Noah had walked away, but God loved the world too much to see it not live according to His love. He started over, but not from scratch. He could have wiped out the whole world, but He didn't. He used one faithful man and his family to begin again because of His *agape* love.

delight |

Think of God's covenant promise to Noah. How does it make you feel to know that God loves you the same way?

How is God asking you to be faithful to Him where you are in life right now?

display |

Has God ever prompted you to do something that felt crazy? Noah definitely knew that feeling. Maybe you've been criticized for making a wise choice when your friends chose to do the opposite. It's not easy to do the right thing, especially when others are watching, but Noah is a great example. Commit to yourself today that you will do the right thing even under pressure. Your faithfulness could have an incredible impact on the people around you!

Take a minute to write out your commitment to do the right thing, no matter what the girls around you might be doing.

Pray that God would give you boldness. If you know some other Christian girls who will stand up for what's right, see if they'll pray for and with you. Ask them to join you as you listen for God's direction and pray for the salvation of those around you.

day 10

COUNTING STARS

---

discover |

READ GENESIS 15:1-6; GENESIS 21:1-5.

He took him outside and said, "Look at the sky and count the stars, if you are able to count them." Then he said to him, "Your offspring will be that numerous."
—*Genesis 15:5*

When you first meet Abram in Genesis 15, he's a man struggling to trust and believe God. He and his wife Sarai have been living in disappointment because they haven't been able to have any children. Back in their day, if you couldn't have children, you were seen as a disgrace. It was a wife's responsibility to not just give her husband children, but to give him a son. God promised to give Abram and Sarai a son, but they were both old and didn't understand how that could possibly happen. This covenant was yet another way of God showing His love to His people.

God can close doors no one else can close, and He can open doors no one else can open.

God doesn't always answer our prayers in the way or the timing that we ask Him. Abram kept trying to find a way to make things happen on his own, outside of God's plan. Even though Abram wasn't perfect, God used Him. In Genesis 17, God made another covenant with Abram and changed his name to Abraham and Sarai's name to Sarah. This is another way that God showed His love for them—He made promises to them that He kept. When Sarah finally had their son Isaac, they laughed and celebrated. Abraham was 100 years old, and Sarah was 90. Nothing is impossible for God!

Abraham's problem was that he was looking at things through his own eyes, not through God's. He couldn't see how God could make any of this work, so he kept second guessing everything. Once he fully put his trust in God, everything changed. He became the father of countless offspring. Because of His love for us, God always keeps His promises.

> Today as you pray, ask God to help you if you're waiting on Him. Ask Him to show you if it's time to move on or time to wait. Pray for friends or family members who may be in a season of waiting right now.

delight |

Is there a door you're waiting on God to open or close in your life? If so, what is it and how long have you been waiting?

Do you ever have trouble believing God will keep His promises? When this has been challenging?

How does God's covenant with Abraham show His love?

display |

Tonight, go outside and look at the stars. As you see countless stars in the sky (hopefully it's a clear night!), let it remind you that God keeps His promises. We just have to trust His timing. He promised Abram a son, and it was decades later that Abraham became a father. What are you waiting on God for right now? Wait patiently. His ways are always better than yours.

day 11

THERE'S ALWAYS GOOD

discover |

READ GENESIS 50:19-21.

"You planned evil against me; God planned it for good to bring about the present result—the survival of many people." —Genesis 50:20

You think you've had some crazy things happen in your life? Look at Joseph. Any one of the events that defined his life seem unimaginable to us, but they're all part of his story. Joseph's life wasn't always a mess. He started out as his father's favorite son out of 12 boys in his family. His brothers were jealous of him, so they sold him into slavery, and he was sent to Egypt. Purchased by Potiphar, the captain of Pharaoh's guard, he was given status and recognition because of his reputation and character. When Potiphar's wife tried to convince him to have an affair with her, he refused, and she accused him of pursuing her when he actually did nothing wrong.

Joseph then spent years in prison and was finally released because of his ability to interpret dreams. He was then made the most influential man in Egypt under Pharaoh and was given great responsibilities and roles. Because of Joseph's wisdom, the Egyptians were spared the effects of a great famine in their land. After decades apart, his brothers came to Egypt looking for help and refuge during the time of famine, and Joseph was able to reveal himself to them. When he let them know who he was, he said, "You planned evil against me; God planned it for good to bring about the present result— the survival of many people." Joseph could see what his brothers couldn't—that God worked good out of a really bad situation. He not only provided for his family's needs, he also forgave them for what they did. God restored their family because of Joseph's faithfulness.

delight |

If you had to face Joseph's trials, how difficult would it be to honor God when it felt like everything was stacked against you?

What's an example in your life of how God has used a bad situation for good?

display |

By this point in your life, someone has hurt you. Next time it happens, remember that you're not responsible for the actions of others, but you are responsible for how you respond. Rather than being quick to respond, ask God to give you patience and wisdom in how you respond to difficult situations you're faced with. Remember that God is always working for your good and His glory, no matter what.

It's easy to want to say negative things about other girls when they hurt us, but God's Word tells us gossip is wrong. Next time you're tempted to start gossiping about someone, write out three positive things about that girl instead. If someone else is gossiping about another girl, stand up for her! It can be as simple as saying, "Hey, I love you, but I think you should talk to her about what's going on." Then, redirect the conversation or walk away if you can't. You don't have to participate just because the girls around you are!

Pray today that God would give you a heart like Joseph's—one ready to forgive, always focused on God, and listening for God's direction. Ask Him to help you be wise in how you respond to difficult circumstances and ready to forgive anyone who has wronged you.

day 12

GO BOLDLY

discover

READ EXODUS 2:11-15; 3:1-10.

"Therefore, go. I am sending you to Pharaoh so that you may lead my people, the Israelites, out of Egypt." —Exodus 3:10

As you journey through the Book of Exodus, Moses is the central character, and his story is complex and compelling. He encounters God on multiple occasions, and he is the one God commanded to lead the Israelites out of Egypt. Moses grew up in Egypt in Pharaoh's household, even though he was a Hebrew boy. Prior to today's passage, we learn that Moses killed an Egyptian, thinking no one saw what he did. When he was confronted, he ran.

We then encounter Moses in Exodus 3, later in his life. An angel of the Lord appeared to him and God spoke to Moses through a burning bush. Can you imagine what that would have been like? God called Moses out to use him as the leader of His plan to rescue the Israelites from Egypt. This was a turning point in Moses' life, and it's a powerful example that God can use anyone.

The love of God is greater than all of our sin. When God called Moses, he said yes. He was an unlikely candidate for the job, but God knew Moses could handle the task at hand and called him to it. Moses wasn't perfect, but God used him anyway.

delight

Have you ever felt like God can't use you because of your sin or past mistakes?

Knowing God loves to use unlikely people to do big things, what's something you believe God may be asking you to do that you feel unqualified for?

How does Moses' story encourage your faith today?

display

Write out the word *go* on a notecard or a sheet of paper. All around the word *go*. write out places, people, and things you feel like God is calling you to "go" to. It could be something you're praying about or something you already know He's called you to do, but put them down on paper today.

As you pray today, praise God that He uses you in spite of your past mistakes and sin. Pray that God would give you courage to step out and do something you might feel unlikely or unqualified to do. Be bold! Don't miss an opportunity God has given you. Listen for the Holy Spirit's leading in your life.

Cherished

day 13

PROTECTED

discover |

READ EXODUS 12:12-16; 21-23.

"I will pass through the land of Egypt on that night and strike every firstborn male in the land of Egypt, both people and animals. I am the LORD; I will execute judgments against all the gods of Egypt. The blood on the houses where you are staying will be a distinguishing mark for you; when I see the blood, I will pass over you. No plague will be among you to destroy you when I strike the land of Egypt." —Exodus 12:12–13

Moses fought for a long time for Pharaoh to release the Israelites from slavery in Egypt. When Pharaoh wouldn't listen, God sent ten plagues on the people, and the last one was responsible for killing all of the firstborn sons in Egypt. Moses warned the Israelites of this and instructed them to sacrifice a lamb and put the blood of the lamb on the doorpost of their home. When they did this, the plague would pass over their house and their son would be spared. The Israelites were God's chosen people, and His hand of protection over them was significant.

This event marks what we now know as Passover. If you've taken an English class recently, you've probably talked about foreshadowing. This story foreshadows the salvation Jesus offers to those who believe in Him. His blood shed on the cross two thousand years ago is what saves us from the sins that would be death to us otherwise. It's up to you whether or not you choose to believe and follow Jesus. When you put your faith in Him, you are covered and guarded by His blood—you are in Christ, and nothing or no one can take that away.

delight |

Has there been a moment in your life when you put your faith in Jesus? Explain.

List all the girls you can think of who need the hope and love of Jesus today.

Why do you think Passover is still so significant today?

Spend a few minutes thanking God for the gift of salvation through Jesus. Praise Him for the love that Jesus expressed toward you as He laid down His life on the cross. Ask Him to reveal people in your life who you can tell about Jesus.

display |

Look back at your list of girls who don't know Jesus. Follow Moses' example and share with them who Jesus is and how they can be saved. Romans 10:9 puts it simply: "If you confess with your mouth, 'Jesus is Lord,' and believe in your heart that God raised him from the dead, you will be saved." Show God's love to those around you this week by sharing the hope of Christ with them. If you don't know how to do this, talk to a youth pastor, small group leader, or other Christian adult in your life and ask for their help.

Cherished

day 14

discover |

READ JOSHUA 1:1-9.

"Haven't I commanded you: be strong and courageous? Do not be afraid or discouraged, for the LORD your God is with you wherever you go." —Joshua 1:9

When Moses died, Joshua had some huge shoes to fill, and he was probably left wondering how to lead. God spoke to him, giving him instructions and encouragement that still encourage us today. God promised His presence, protection, and territory for Joshua to lead the people toward. He told Joshua on several occasions to "be strong and courageous." God wasn't going to send Joshua anywhere alone, and He reminded Joshua to keep the instructions Moses gave him. Joshua was well-prepared to lead, and God promised His loving presence would be with Joshua, even though Moses wasn't there anymore.

When things change, it's easy to get thrown off and lose your way. Joshua had been dependent on Moses' leadership and relationship with God and found himself in charge without his mentor. It would have been so easy for Joshua to either take the reins and lead however he wanted or to run away scared because he couldn't live up to Moses' legacy. Thankfully, Joshua didn't do either one of those things, but he became a man of courage who boldly led the Israelites into the promised land. He was equipped for the thing God called him to do, and he ran with it. The kindness and love of God gave him the courage to do hard things.

As you spend a few minutes praying, ask God to give you courage and boldness like He gave Joshua. Thank God that He promises to go with you and before you as you walk with Him.

delight |

Describe a situation in your life where you need some courage right now.

How does God's promise to be with Joshua—no matter what they faced—help you understand God's character?

How can you honor God in the midst of changing circumstances?

display |

Change is hard, but God is good in the midst of it all. If you're not in the middle of a change, maybe a friend or family member is. Write them a note, send a text, or make a phone call to encourage them today. Pray that God would give them courage and boldness like Joshua.

Use an app to create a fun lock-screen of the words *God is with me wherever I go*. Set it as your background, and every time you see it, praise God for being with you always.

day 15

UNLIKELY KING

---

discover

READ 1 SAMUEL 16:1-13.

But the LORD said to Samuel, "Do not look at his appearance or his stature because I have rejected him. Humans do not see what the LORD sees, for humans see what is visible, but the LORD sees the heart." —1 Samuel 16:7

Are you starting to see the theme that God uses people no one else might have used? It's crazy that Scripture tells us David didn't stand out in a major way and was short. God encouraged Samuel to look past David's exterior to his heart. If you know much about David's story, you know he became King of Israel and was known as the man after God's own heart (Acts 13:22). David made mistakes, but we see God continue to use him because his eyes were so fixed on God. He wrote much of the book of Psalms, and you can see his prayers and praises through the good and bad times as you explore that powerful book.

David's heart was what set him apart from everyone else. Samuel came to anoint the next King, and all of his brothers looked like better candidates than David did. What you can learn from this is that God doesn't always call the most likely person, but He always prepares them for the task in front of them. Your heart is the most important part of you. Scripture says it's the wellspring of your very life (Prov. 4:23), and our job is to keep our hearts tender toward God and His unconditional love for us.

delight |

When have you felt like the unlikely choice for something? Explain.

How does it change your perspective to know that God uses unlikely people to do big things?

display |

You may think that because you're a teen girl, God doesn't have a purpose or plan for your life yet. That couldn't be further from the truth! God called out David as a young boy to be anointed as the next King to lead His people. It's never too early for God to plant those plans inside of you and begin to work on your heart, so don't miss out! Pray that God would begin to show you how He's preparing you for the future. He has great plans for you and He loves you!

Think about a time when you've looked at another girl whose appearance made you judge her harshly. But God sees things differently; she has value, no matter how she may dress or look. Whenever you're tempted to think poorly of another girl, say to yourself: *God sees her heart, so I should, too.*

> Thank God that He has plans for your life that you can't even see yet. As you begin to realize this, pray that you would walk with your head held high into whatever those things are. Being a middle or high school student isn't easy, but you're not alone. Pray that God would surround you with like-minded friends who can encourage you when it gets hard.

Cherished

day 16

WISDOM REIGNS

discover

READ 1 KINGS 3:5-14.

"So give your servant a receptive heart to judge your people and to discern between good and evil. For who is able to judge this great people of yours?" Now it pleased the LORD that Solomon had requested this. —1 Kings 3:9-10

Solomon was the son of King David. He was a young man when his dad died and he became king. God spoke to him through a dream and said, "Ask. What should I give you?" (v. 5). In a big move for such a young leader, Solomon asked for wisdom.

He could have asked for power, a long life, happiness, money, or anything else you can think of, but he asked for wisdom. He knew what being king required because he watched his dad be a powerful, influential leader. Solomon was aware that the job wasn't easy, but he was ready to do it because he knew God loved him and would be with him. This passage tells us that Solomon's request was pleasing to God, and it led God to bless Solomon beyond giving him the wisdom he requested.

When we ask for things that honor God, He is pleased and shows us His love. God will always give you what you need, but sometimes He's waiting for you to ask. Once you've been given these good gifts from God, the expectation is that you'll steward them well. Solomon wasn't perfect, but he used his wisdom to be a powerful, influential king like his dad.

delight |

What do you think would look different in your life if God gave you wisdom like Solomon?

What situation in your life could use some godly wisdom?

How are you stewarding the gifts God has given you?

display |

If you had one "wish," what would you wish for? Solomon was given this opportunity and asked God for wisdom. If you're being honest, wisdom might not be very high on your list. Solomon's example shows you that wisdom should be something we pray and ask God for on a regular basis. When's the last time you asked for wisdom? Start today, and ask God to make you wise as you go about your day and week.

Pray for the other Christian girls you know to seek and live out God's wisdom. Then, prayerfully ask one of those girls to hold you accountable to pursue godly wisdom in all things.

> Today, pray for wisdom like Solomon. Pray that God would help you learn how to make wise decisions and that you would be a wise friend to the girls around you.

day 17

VICTORY

discover |

READ 1 KINGS 18:20-39.

Then the LORD's fire fell and consumed the burnt offering, the wood, the stones, and the dust, and it licked up the water that was in the trench. When all the people saw it, they fell facedown and said, "The LORD, he is God! The LORD, he is God!" —1 Kings 18:38-39

Elijah was an Old Testament prophet God used in some really interesting ways. In today's passage, Elijah challenged the people to choose whether they were going to worship God or Baal. He challenged Baal's prophets to a dueling sacrifice—they would get the first chance to call on the name of their god and see if he would light their altar on fire. There were 450 of them, so it seemed like a simple request. Elijah sought to reveal which god was real by seeing which one made their presence known. All along, Elijah knew His God would win.

After a period of silence from Baal, it was Elijah's turn to call on his God. Elijah made the challenge more interesting by having his altar completely drenched with water three times. When was the last time you saw something wet catch on fire? Never! He knew that God could do it, even when the circumstances didn't seem favorable. As today's passage shows, God got all of the glory, and the people understood who the one true God is. None of this was Elijah's doing; it was all about God showing His unconditional love toward Elijah and the people who needed to know Him.

delight |

In what area of your life has God clearly given you a victory you can celebrate?

How do you like to celebrate a win?

Elijah asked God to do the impossible. When was the last time you asked God to do something that seemed impossible? What was it?

display |

It's easy to feel God's love when things are going well, but it's much more difficult when life gets complicated. The victory God brought for Elijah was huge—not just for Elijah, but for all of the Baal worshipers who wouldn't believe God until then. When you experience a victory in your own life, celebrate and enjoy what God has given you!

Name one victory God has given you recently, then name one girl you can share with and celebrate. Make a point to celebrate that win this month!

Pray that God would show you how to point victories back to Him. Pray for courage like Elijah had when he asked God to do something that seemed impossible.

day 18

WHEN THE GOING GETS ROUGH

---

discover |

READ 1 KINGS 19:1-18.

Then he said, "Go out and stand on the mountain in the LORD's presence." At that moment, the LORD passed by. A great and mighty wind was tearing at the mountains and was shattering cliffs before the LORD, but the LORD was not in the wind. After the wind there was an earthquake, but the LORD was not in the earthquake. After the earthquake there was a fire, but the LORD was not in the fire. And after the fire there was a voice, a soft whisper. When Elijah heard it, he wrapped his face in his mantle and went out and stood at the entrance of the cave. Suddenly, a voice came to him and said, "What are you doing here, Elijah?"
—1 Kings 19:11-13

Elijah's story took a quick turn when Jezebel— the evil queen of Israel—threatened his life. Right after a victory, Elijah's life was on the line. Isn't it crazy how fast things can change? He ran and prayed that God would just take him right then and there. An angel came to Elijah and led him on a journey to meet with God. Today's key verses tell the story of when Elijah was waiting on God to meet with him. Elijah expected God to come in a loud way, but He came in a quiet whisper. The Lord gave him instructions and sent him on his way. Elijah's faithfulness to God was evident throughout his life, but this wasn't an easy situation.

There's a good chance Elijah had a hard time following the angel's instructions. He barely got to celebrate his victory over the prophets of Baal before someone was trying to kill him. Have you ever felt that way? You can barely soak in the goodness of a win in your life before something comes crashing down. You have to remember that God's unconditional love reigns supreme in both the good times and the hard times. Nothing catches Him off guard, and He's always in control.

delight |

Have you ever faced a difficult situation right after a really good one? Explain.

What's one way you can remind yourself of God's *agape* love for you when times are tough?

How can you listen for God's voice, even when it's quiet?

display |

When things are tough, it doesn't mean God loves you any less. It just means there's a different way for Him to get glory through your life than you might have thought. You have to trust what you know, not what you feel. You've seen God's faithfulness in your life, so don't forget it! Remind yourself that God is the same—He never changes. He is for you and with you wherever you go.

Using a dry-erase marker on your mirror or some fun colored markers on card stock, write out the phrase, *God is the same—always*. Every time you see this phrase, remember that God never changes; He has always loved you and He always will.

> Pray that God would give you the quiet you need to hear His voice when He's guiding you. Ask God to remind you of His faithfulness in your life so you won't forget. Pray for wisdom when the tough times come, and commit to trusting what you know instead of what you feel.

day 19

NEVER TOO FAR

━━━━━

discover |

READ JONAH 3.

God saw their actions—that they had turned from their evil ways—so God relented from the disaster he had threatened them with. And he did not do it.
—Jonah 3:10

From the outside looking in, the people of Nineveh didn't deserve what God gave them. They were evil people who had no regard for God. God chose the prophet Jonah to take His message to the people of Nineveh, but Jonah decided he didn't want any part of that plan. He took off in the opposite direction, but God wouldn't let him go. When he finally arrived in Nineveh—after getting swallowed by a giant fish and living in its belly for a few days— Jonah prophesied to the people, and they listened.

The people repented of their sins, fasted, and prayed. We see that "God saw their actions—that they had turned from their evil ways—so God relented from the disaster he had threatened them with. And he did not do it." Jonah's obedience led to their salvation. Jonah was a messenger of hope to the Ninevites.

So often we see God pursue those He knows are headed in the wrong direction. There's no person or group of people too far off course for God's unconditional love. He's always there—waiting, pursuing, and ready. God loved them right where they were and sent Jonah as His messenger to help them understand.

delight |

There's no one God won't chase after with His unconditional love. How does this truth change your perspective on God's love? Explain.

What should your response be when God calls you out on your sin?

display |

Is there a girl in your life that you think is too far from God to ever know Him? Maybe God has sent you to be a Jonah in her life—the one who proclaims truth to her. If nothing else, start praying for her. Your job is to love her the way God loves her and show who He is to her. Be faithful to do your part, and let God's unconditional love do the rest.

Pray for an open heart toward those who seem to be far from God. Ask God to show you a girl you can be a messenger of hope to this week. Ask God for wisdom and help as you keep your eyes open.

day 20

IN THE FIRE

discover |

READ DANIEL 3.

Then King Nebuchadnezzar jumped up in alarm. He said to his advisers, "Didn't we throw three men, bound, into the fire?'" "Yes, of course, Your Majesty," they replied to the king. He exclaimed, "Look! I see four men, not tied, walking around in the fire unharmed; and the fourth looks like a son of the gods."
—Daniel 3:24-25

Three men were thrown into the fire for being obedient to God, and they didn't burn up. This is a crazy story! What's even crazier is that eyewitnesses saw another man in the fire with them. God's unconditional love extends to all who display their love for Him for others to see. He loves us and is present with us in the fires of our lives. You may not be able to see His physical presence, but He is with you.

Let's back up a little bit. King Nebuchadnezzar ordered all of his people to worship a god he created, but Shadrach, Meshach, and Abednego all refused to worship anything but the one true God. They were called to come before the king and again stood firm, telling him they wouldn't worship the god he made. Nebuchadnezzar was furious. These men were confident that God was with them and would help them, no matter what. This opened the king's eyes to see God's power and authority, but it took the boldness of these three men to show him.

delight |

How can you take a stand for Jesus this week?

Who are some girls that can stand with you? If you can't think of any, pray that God would send you some like-minded girls to stand with you.

display |

There's a good chance you've done something in your life because "everyone else is doing it." It's so easy to fall into peer pressure because it can be easier to fit in than to stand out. Throughout the Bible, God gives examples of people who went against what everyone else was doing and stood out because they knew He would be standing with them. It's time to be bold and stand up. If you've been waiting to see who else is going to be the first one to make a stand for Jesus, maybe everyone else is doing the same thing, and you need to be the first one. Even when it's scary, Jesus promises to be with you.

Pray today for boldness. God has placed you right where you are on purpose, so pray that He shows you how you can make an impact for Him right where you are. Pray that you have opportunities to show the love of God with the people God has placed in your life.

day 21

BOLD

discover |

READ ESTHER 4.

"If you keep silent at this time, relief and deliverance will come to the Jewish people from another place, but you and your father's family will be destroyed. Who knows, perhaps you have come to your royal position for such a time as this."
—Esther 4:14

Esther was in a unique position, and God used her because she was willing to risk it all for what was most important. She was from a Jewish background and became a very unlikely queen. Esther had the opportunity to stand up for her people when they were being persecuted and risked her life to ask the king to save them. Women weren't given opportunities like this back in her day, but her relative, Mordecai, reminded her that maybe this was the exact reason she became queen!

She took an unbelievable risk to even go speak to the king when he hadn't called her to see him. It was a life or death decision, but she knew it was worth it to do the right thing and plead for the lives of the Jews. She asked Mordecai to have them fast and pray for her leading up to her meeting with the king and went boldly to speak to him.

This book of the Bible is really interesting because the name of God is never mentioned, but His love for Esther is very evident. God protected her when she could have easily been executed. He gave her courage when she needed it most, and gave her favor with the king when she pleaded for the Jews to be spared. God's presence was clearly seen in her and through her.

delight |

What's something you believe God has uniquely positioned you to do?

List the names of some girls in your life who will pray for you when you need it.

How do you see God's love for you displayed in your life?

display |

Sometimes God will call you to step out of your comfort zone and take a risk. When those moments arise, write them down. Make sure they line up with what the Bible says. God won't ever call you to do something that doesn't line up with His character. If you don't keep a journal of prayer requests, now is a great time to start. Whether you write them in a journal, a note on your phone, or somewhere else—track what you're praying for and what God is guiding you to do.

As you spend time in prayer today, ask God to give you opportunities to be bold and stand up for what's right. Pray that you would have peace as you face opposition and that you would point others to God by doing what He's called you to do.

day 22

STAND UP

discover |

READ NEHEMIAH 1.

Please, LORD, let your ear be attentive to the prayer of your servant and to that of your servants who delight to revere your name. Give your servant success today, and grant him compassion in the presence of this man.
—Nehemiah 1:11

Nehemiah's story is similar to Esther's because he also had the ear of the King. As the cupbearer to the king, he was responsible for making sure nothing poisonous was given to the king, so he drank everything before the king did and put his life on the line every day. At the time of today's passage, the Jews were in exile away from Jerusalem. After hearing a report from home, he felt led to go back and rebuild the walls of Jerusalem. His people were in trouble, and he was the one God called to take on this massive task. The goal was restoration, and Nehemiah felt called to take the weight of it on his shoulders.

The way Nehemiah knew what to do was through prayer and fasting. Throughout the Bible, it's evident that God restores those He loves, and it was no different with Nehemiah and his people. He repented of his sins and reminded God of the promises He made to Moses. He asked God for success and compassion when he met with the king, and the Lord's favor was very evident. Nehemiah's prayerful approach showed his love for God, and God's response showed His love for Nehemiah.

delight |

Describe a time when you went to God before you dealt with a tough situation.

How have you seen God's love for you in a specific way?

Is there anything in your life that needs to get out of the way (like how Nehemiah repented of his sins) before you ask God for something?

display |

Is there something in your life that needs restoring? It could be a friendship, a relationship with a family member, or a teacher or coach you need to apologize to. How could owning up to whatever went wrong and asking God to restore things change the situation?

List two steps you will take toward restoration in a relationship this week.

Pray that God would give you insight to restore anything in your life that needs mending, whether it's big or small. Pray honestly and intentionally, modeling your prayer after the one Nehemiah prayed.

day 23

NO FEAR

discover |

READ LUKE 1:26-38.

"See, I am the Lord's servant," said Mary. "May it happen to me as you have said." Then the angel left her. — Luke 1:38

Did you know that Mary was a teen when God told her she would become the mother of Jesus? At your age, can you imagine what that would be like? It would probably create some feelings of panic, anxiety, and fear. It was a huge responsibility to bear, and one that no one had ever gone through before or since.

Throughout the Bible, God reminds people of two things:

- Don't fear.

- I am with you.

These so clearly show His love for those He spoke to, and Mary was no exception. He again chose someone ordinary to do something extraordinary through. Her story led into the birth of the One who would most clearly reveal God's *agape* love to the whole world. This was no easy task, yet she accepted it with courage when she said, "... I am the Lord's servant. May it happen to me as you have said." She recognized God's love for her, and it led her to trust Him completely even though the news she was receiving from the angel would change her life—and the world—forever.

delight |

Knowing that God will be with you no matter what, is there something you'd be more bold and courageous to do?

God used Mary as a teen to do something incredibly significant. How does that encourage you that God can use you right where you are?

God's love for Mary was shown by His presence with her. Have you felt God's love through His presence? Explain.

display |

The passage you read today shows that nothing is impossible with God. It's easy to become disappointed or frustrated when life doesn't go like you thought it would, but so often it's because it's not God's best. When God is in the middle of any situation, and you're listening for His voice, nothing is impossible. Today, share with a godly girl friend about an area of fear in your life, whether it feels big or small. Pray together that God would give you His strength as you face whatever it is that's in front of you.

As you pray today, ask God to give you faith like Mary to believe that He can work in and through your life. Pray for whatever area of fear you identified and ask God to be with you as you face it.

Cherished

"Haven't I commanded you: be strong and courageous?

Do not be afraid or discouraged, for the Lord your God is with you wherever you go."

JOSHUA 1:9

Tip: Set a timer for one minute. Say the verse and reference aloud as many times as you can. Do this a few days in a row until you have the verse memorized.

day 24

WITH EVERYTHING

discover |

READ LUKE 10:25-27, DEUTERONOMY 6:4-9.

"Love the Lord your God with all your heart, with all your soul, with all your strength, and with all your mind ..." —Luke 10:27a

God loves you, but you must also love Him. You've seen examples of stories throughout the Bible that show how God has expressed His love over time, but it's critical that you see how important it is to love Him in return. He doesn't just want part of your heart—He wants all of it. This passage in Luke 10 says, "Love the Lord your God with all your heart, with all your soul, with all your strength, and with all your mind," and He means it. You're to love Him with every part of your being.

In the verses you read in Deuteronomy, you saw that this thought wasn't new when Jesus said it, but came from the Old Testament. After Moses gave the Israelites the Ten Commandments, these are other laws he gave them as well. He encouraged them that this is the greatest commandment, and they were to put it in a visible place in their home, and on their hand and forehead. He wanted to make sure they didn't forget.

delight |

In what areas of your life is it easy to love God and give Him everything?

In what areas of your life is it tough to love God and give Him everything?

Is there an area of your life you know needs to change so you can love God with everything? Explain.

display |

Can others see Jesus in you? If someone were to ask your family members and friends if you knew Jesus, what would they say? Do you love God with everything? It's more than just wearing a cross necklace, a Jesus t-shirt, or posting about God on social media from time to time. It's about letting every part of your life reflect who He is. Let it show; don't be ashamed. Write down one evidence in your life of your love for Jesus.

Pray that you're able to show the love of Jesus with everything you have and everything you are. If there are parts of your life you've been holding back, today is a great day to surrender those things to God. Confess to Him that you need His help and you're ready to love Jesus with your whole heart.

day 25

WHO'S YOUR NEIGHBOR?

discover |

READ LUKE 10:25-37.

"... and your neighbor as yourself." —Luke 10:27b

Today's reading picks up where you left off yesterday. Jesus adds to the passage found in Deuteronomy 6, saying "love your neighbor as yourself." Maybe you're wondering who your neighbor is (so did the guy who asked Jesus). It's anyone in your life—not just the people who live next door to you. In this story, a Jewish man needs help, and only one person stops to help him, a Samaritan. Jews and Samaritans couldn't stand each other, but this man didn't let that get in the way when he saw someone who needed help. Are you willing to love your neighbors that way?

The good Samaritan set his personal feelings aside to help someone who needed him. Who needs you? Maybe there's a girl at school, a sibling, or a former friend who isn't easy to love. Rather than just turning away from them, how can you love and serve them well? Jesus had compassion for those who opposed Him, and loved them just like anyone else.

delight

Who are the girls in your life that are difficult to love?

What's holding you back from loving your neighbor no matter what?

List a few ways you can love your neighbors.

display |

As you learn to love your neighbor as yourself, think about who you need to tell about Jesus. Think about it this way. Fast forward 15 years. You run into a girl from school who can't wait to tell you something—they've just started a relationship with Jesus and want to tell you all about Him. You respond by saying, "I've known Jesus since I was a kid." They look back at you and say, "Why didn't you tell me?" One of the biggest ways you can show love for your neighbor is by telling her about Jesus. What's stopping you from doing that today for the people around you?

Write the names of two girls you plan to share Jesus with this month.

Today, pray for the people in your life that are hard to love. Ask God to let you see them the way He sees them and that your heart toward them would change. Pray for opportunities to show God's love to your neighbors, whether they're strangers or friends.

Cherished

day 26

LOVE YOUR ENEMY

discover |

READ MATTHEW 5:43-44; JOHN 17:14-26.

"You have heard that it was said, Love your neighbor and hate your enemy. But I tell you, love your enemies and pray for those who persecute you..."
—Matthew 5:43-44

These verses sound so backwards. Love your enemies? Pray for those who persecute you? It's so opposite of what the world tells you. Neither of these things is easy to do, but Jesus didn't call you to do easy things. Jesus lived an upside down kind of life, and He's calling you to do the same. It may not feel like the cool thing to do, but it's what Jesus was always found doing.

Jesus often put Himself right in the path of those who were considered His enemies, and He loved them right where they were. When Jesus died on the cross, He didn't just die for those who were His friends, but those who would also call themselves His enemies. Don't believe it? Look at what Jesus said in Luke 23:34 as He hung on the cross. Jesus prayed that they would know His Father, that God would forgive for what they were doing, and that they would spend eternity in heaven with Him. He showed kindness, grace, and mercy to people—even those who were actively killing Him. What a Savior we have!

delight |

Why is it so hard to love your enemies?

Who do you need to spend some time loving and praying for?

How does Jesus' response to His enemies and persecutors challenge you?

display |

One of the greatest things you can do for a girl who's difficult to love is pray for her. There's a really good chance that your heart will change and you won't look at her the same way anymore. Jesus loved everyone He encountered and set an incredible example for the way we should live. Write down the name of a girl you need to pray for, even if it's difficult.

Today may be a really hard day for you to pray. It's not easy to pray for those who are in some way your enemy. Even if it's just saying their name as you pray, know that you're honoring Jesus in your prayer. Continue to speak their name over the next few days and see if God begins to change your heart. Pray for opportunities to show God's love to them.

Cherished

day 27

TRUE FRIENDSHIP

discover |

READ JOHN 15:9-17.

"No one has greater love than this: to lay down his life for his friends."
—John 15:13

What makes a true friend? It's more than just the person you text the most or who you spend the most time with outside of school. It's the one who knows you—like, really knows you. They know more than just your favorite team or Starbucks drink. They know what hurts you, what matters to you, and what you're all about. Your real friends are the ones you can be yourself with. You're the same around them as you are around everyone else, and you've let them into your life.

True friendship is hard to come by but incredibly valuable when you find it. In this passage, Jesus was talking to His disciples the night before He was crucified. He was encouraging them to love each other well because He loved them well. True friends love one another, and they're willing to do whatever it takes to love each other, as long as it honors Jesus.

Jesus was preparing them that He was about to lay down His life for them, and that they should be willing to do the same for others. Does it mean that you have to literally lay your life down? No, but it means that you should be willing to do whatever you can to love your friends well.

delight |

What does true friendship mean to you?

How are you a true friend to people in your life?

Which girls in your life would consider you to be a true friend?

display |

How can you love your friends well? Show up for them. Cheer them on. Encourage them when things are hard. Point them to Jesus with your words and your actions. Defend them when you need to. What can you do today to love one of your friends well? Here are a few ideas: send a passage of Scripture and let them know you're praying for them, write a note or card, show up for a game, or let them know you think they're awesome. Get creative!

Pray today that God would give you some true friends and that you would grow in being a true friend to others. Ask God to give you opportunities to love the friends in your life well. Pray that you would be willing to help and stand up for them however you can.

day 28

SHOW HONOR

discover

READ ROMANS 12:9-18.

Love one another deeply as brothers and sisters. Take the lead in honoring one another. —Romans 12:10

What does it mean to honor one another? It's rooted in respect and putting others before yourself. As you've learned or been reminded what it means to love one another, this is your challenge: don't just love others, lead in loving others. Be gracious and kind. Honor God by honoring others. This doesn't mean you're supposed to be a doormat that gets stepped on, but you're willing to serve and put the needs of others before your own.

This passage encourages you to live at peace with others and to surround yourself with humble people. The world is telling you to do the opposite. The world says to put yourself first, and that the louder you are, the more respected you'll be. Love others the way Jesus would—with grace and patience. Jesus set the bar high and expects us to do our best to show honor to the people we encounter, whether we know them or not.

If you have trouble doing this because you lack respect for people in your life, remember that Jesus loves you when you don't deserve it. He laid down His life for us, even when we were dead in our sins and set against Him. If He would do that for us, the least we should do is be willing to show honor to our brothers and sisters in Christ.

delight |

Think of a time when you've shown honor to someone, and write about it in the space provided.

How does it feel when others show you honor?

What does it truly mean to you to honor people around you?

display |

Showing honor may sound old fashioned, but it's the way Jesus led and lived. How can you show honor to those around you? Whether it's your parents, friends from school, neighbors, siblings, or someone else in your life, how can you love them well by honoring them? Challenge yourself to show honor intentionally every day for the next week. Think ahead of some ways you can do this, but also see how God leads you in the moments you aren't expecting. Write one idea below.

Ask God for the opportunity to honor people in your life. Pray that He would show you how to live this out one day at a time and one person at a time. Pray for eyes to see other people the way Jesus sees them—with love, compassion, and kindness.

day 29

discover |

READ 1 JOHN 2:15-17.

Do not love the world or the things in the world. If anyone loves the world, the love of the Father is not in him. —1 John 2:15

The world wants your attention and your affection. It's clever and crafty, and sometimes you won't even see it coming. There's a distinct line between loving the world and loving God, and this passage is a clear reminder of where your love and loyalty should lie. When you begin to love the things of the world, you are no longer loving God the way you're intended to. You can't do both at the same time—it just isn't possible. One will always win out.

At some point, you have to make a decision about who you are and whose you are. The more you get into God's Word and fall in love with Jesus, the less you'll look like the world. The things that used to be important to you will shift, and it'll be easier to figure out what's true and what's a lie. Things that seem as innocent as the music you listen to, the social media apps you spend time on, video games you play, or TV shows you watch all show what and who you love.

> **Pray that your love for God will be able to stand up against the things of this world. Distraction and temptation get in the way so quickly, and it's never too early to start standing up for what's right. Pray that God would give you boldness and confidence to look more like Him each day.**

delight |

How is the love of the Father evident in you?

Name a few things in your life that look more like the world than Jesus.

What strategy can you use to love the world less and love Jesus more?

display |

Looking less like the world and more like Jesus is a lifelong process, so don't panic if you can't immediately turn everything around. It's all about constantly moving in the right direction, which is toward God. The things of the world that will tempt you and try to gain your affection will change in different seasons of your life, so now is a great time to start being accountable to some godly girls and a trusted adult leader who loves Jesus. They'll be able to spot things in your life that you can't see and will be able to pray for you and encourage you along the way.

Cherished

day 30

discover |

READ JOHN 13:31-35.

"I give you a new command: Love one another. Just as I have loved you, you are also to love one another. By this everyone will know that you are my disciples, if you love one another." —John 13:34-35

We love because Jesus loved us first. As we live in light of His unconditional love for us, we have to remember that He loves everyone—not just the people who are like us or share our perspectives and views. The thing about Jesus is that He never leaves people where they are; He always pushes them to change and become more like Him. He doesn't expect us to come to Him perfect, but we should leave different after we experience and know Him.

You've had the chance to reflect on this in a few ways this month, but do other people know you love Jesus by your words and actions? Do they know you love Him by your love? When you show love to those around you, people identify you with Jesus, and you're showing them what it really looks like to be a Christ follower. It's only because of Jesus that we're able to love people well. It's more than just regular love—it's a love that sacrifices, puts others first, and honors people. Don't miss the opportunities that are right in front of you to show the *agape* love that you've been shown.

delight |

What's a specific way you can show the love of Jesus to one girl who needs it?

How have you been shown the love of Jesus by someone? What did it mean to you to be shown this type of love?

Do people know you love Jesus by your love? Why or why not?

display |

Let love be what you're known for. Let that love point people to Jesus and the truth so that others can see Him in you. Don't miss the opportunities that are right in front of you—at school, with your family, on the court or field, on the stage, behind your instrument, or wherever else you might be. Because of Jesus' unconditional love for you, choose today to love others the way He loves them. List one way you can show *agape* love to someone today.

> Jesus, let me love you in a way that shows everyone I come into contact with who I am and whose I am. Let your love for me spill out into all of my relationships so that I'm loving others with the kind of love you've given me. Let me be a person who takes your unconditional love wherever you need me to go. Amen.

"I give you a new command: Love one another. Just as I have loved you, you are also to love one another.

By this
everyone will
know that
you are my
disciples, if
you love one
another."

JOHN 13:34-35

Tip: Print out the verse in a large, outline font. Color in
each word of the verse, saying it aloud as you go. Or, if
you enjoy hand lettering, grab a sheet of card stock, cut
of pallet wood, or a dry-erase board and write out your
verse creatively. Read the verse aloud when you finish.

Unconditionally
What We Know of It

We toss around the word love without truly knowing what it means, especially when it comes to unconditional love. There are songs about it, movies that make us feel like we know it, and books that describe it with vivid imagery.

How would you describe love in your own words? What about unconditional love?

When you're trying to figure out what a word means, it can be helpful to break down the different parts of the word. Take the word *unconditional*, for example. The prefix, un means "not," and the word *conditional* means "dependent upon a premise or provision." So, when we put these two together, the word *unconditional* essentially means "not dependent upon a premise or provision." Put simply, there are no strings attached and no standards that must be met as a prerequisite or requirement for this thing. When speaking of unconditional love, this means nothing is required of us to earn this love; we don't have to meet specific standards before we are loved; and we are loved first regardless of who we are or what we have done.

But we all have those days when we feel like something should disqualify us from being loved, right? Especially when it comes to God's love.

Think about your own life and relationship with love. Now, write out five things or events that have made you feel unlovable, rejected, unworthy, or alone, leaving room at the beginning of each statement.

1.

2.

3.

4.

5.

Now, in a different color of pen or marker, go back and rewrite each statement, using the phrase "God loves me even when..."

How God Loves Us

In the Bible, the word *agape* is used to describe God's unconditional love. It is often used interchangeably with the word *phileo* (love for other believers) in reference to God's love for His Son or a believer or Jesus' love for His followers.[1]

Read Matthew 19:19; John 3:35; 13:23; 14:21; 1 Corinthians 13; and Colossians 3:12-16. In 10 words or less, summarize what these passages—together—tell you about God's Word.

What this Means for Us

God's *agape* love means we're loved more deeply than we can ever understand—by the God of the universe, no less! But God's absolute and unconditional love for us reveals to us something about the way we should love others. God is the source of any true and biblical love and the only way we're able to love others well. Scripture made this truth evident in John 13:34: "Just as I have loved you, you also are to love one another."

Examine your heart. How might your interactions with others need to change so you can show them God's *agape* love?

List three ways you can show God's *agape* love to others this week. Don't focus on the general "how I can love others" tips, but focus on specific people in your life and specific ways you personally can show them love.

Cherished

Tough Love: How God's Love Corrects Us

Who doesn't love being complimented, encouraged, or told that we're amazing? The Bible even says that kind words "are like a honeycomb, sweetness to the soul and health to the body" (Prov. 16:24). But kind words don't need to be overdone, meaning we don't need to stretch the truth to speak kindness. We are also called to speak "the truth in love" (Eph. 4:15). Our culture imperfectly describes this concept as tough love. Essentially, tough love means doing what's best for others, whether or not they recognize our actions as loving.

It's so easy to think love is always a feel-good, corny paper valentine card and candy hearts, inspirational speeches and Nicholas Sparks level love letters kind of deal. But the truth is that love often carries both joy and pain, sometimes at the same time. To get a better feel for how these feelings coexist within love, think about God sending Jesus to die for us in such an excruciating and humiliating way. Scripture says this is how we know love (1 John 3:16).

God did all of this to provide a way for us to have a restored relationship with Him. But committing our lives to Him doesn't stop with the sinner's prayer. Being fully committed to God means that we make a decision to follow Him and then we live it out. Our lives change forever for the better. Each day that we follow Jesus, living in complete obedience to Him, we become more like Him. This is called sanctification—a process that continues for the rest of our lives.

We like "yes" people (those who won't tell us we're wrong and think everything we do is awesome) and love stories where the hero will go to any lengths to win the affections of the heroine, constantly telling her how wonderful she is. Now, God went to great lengths for us and through His Word, time and time again, He communicates to us our value and worth as His children. But He isn't a "yes" God. He tells us the truth and how to live our lives seeking His best for us—and that includes discipline. Let's take a look at what Scripture has to say.

Fill in the blanks to guide your understanding as you read Hebrews 12:4-11.

Paul tells us not to take "the _____ _____ lightly" or to "lose heart when" He _____ us (v. 5). God _____ those He _____, and _____ His children (v. 6). We must _____ ourselves to endure _____ as God's _____ (v. 7).

God disciplines us so we can "share his _____" (v. 10).

Discipline never seems _____ when it occurs, but _____. But it trains us, and in the process, yields the "_____ _____ ___ _____ (v. 11)"

Girls, it's important to note that when it says "God is dealing with you as sons" (v. 7), this doesn't exclude you. The "sons of God" refers to all children of God. In the New Testament times when Paul wrote these words, sons received their fathers' inheritance; they were legally the heirs of all their fathers owned. By designating all children of God as sons, then, Paul indicates here that women have just as much of a right to their inheritance as children of God.[2]

God disciplines, reproves (corrects), and punishes His children. Why? Just like a good earthly father, God tells us "no" for our good. Through every "no," or "not that way," or "not like that" God teaches us the right way. Every time God disciplines, reproves, or punishes, He is sanctifying us.

Yes, when we mess up, God will discipline us—but that's because He loves us. He often allows us to experience the consequences of our mistakes. But that doesn't mean He extends any less grace, any less mercy, or any less love. Instead, if God disciplines us, He is molding us even more into His image. His "tough love" is still His absolute, unconditional love for us as His children.

List some ways God's "tough love" has changed your life for the better.

How did you experience His discipline in the moment?

What are some ways you can speak the truth in love to someone who is suffering as a result of her sin?

Cherished

You're Speaking My Language: How to Communicate Love

All people need love; it's key to healthy spiritual, emotional, mental, and physical development. Love is essential to your overall health and happiness. While romantic love can certainly be an ingredient of the love we receive, it can also be familial love, the love of friends, or the love of caring others (like teachers, counselors, pastors, or student pastors). Simply put: You don't have to be "in love" to experience love.

The truth is, although all people need (and deeply desire) to be loved, not all people give or receive love the same way. According to Dr. Gary Chapman, author of The 5 Love Languages®, people receive love in five main ways: words of affirmation, quality time, physical touch, acts of service, and gifts. Here's the basic gist of what each of these means:

- **Words of affirmation.** This can mean receiving encouragement or praise, whether verbally, through a hand-written note, or even through a text message.

- **Quality time.** Those who love quality time don't just want you to be around them for an hour and consider it good, they want your undivided attention for however long you happen to be with them, doing something they love. Eye contact and reaffirming that they are heard will be important.

- **Receiving Gifts.** You love receiving gifts—no matter how big or small. You also really appreciate the thought, time, and effort someone puts into a gift.

- **Acts of Service.** People who "speak" this love language feel valued and loved when others do nice things for them. You might grab your best friend's coffee when you're out or do the dishes for your dad—but you'll speak straight to their hearts no matter how simple the act may seem.

- **Physical touch.** This isn't exclusive to romantic hand-holding. Someone with this love language might just appreciate a hug or a gentle touch to the shoulder while you're talking.[3]

If you're not sure what your primary love language is, you can take a fast and free quiz here: https://www.5lovelanguages.com/quizzes/teen-quiz/.

What is your love language? (Even if you don't take the free quiz, you can simply respond with the one that sounds most like you based on the descriptions.)

When do you feel the most loved and valued?

You might know or might just have to guess, but what do you think the love languages are for your best friends, immediate family, or boyfriend?

Jot down a few ideas for how you can show love to each of these people this week.

Now, take a minute and write out how you might show love to someone who "speaks" each of these love languages over the next month. Get specific!

Our God is a God of love who wants His people to love one another as He has loved us (1 John 4:19). In fact, this is one way Jesus even said the rest of the world will know we belong to Him (John 13:35). While you can certainly show love any of these ways, knowing how a person best receives love comes only through time and effort invested in the relationship. As you get to know the girl next to you—yes, even the one who's difficult to love—pay attention to what makes her really light up! Then, make an effort to let her know she is loved. You never know how one word of affirmation, one real and raw hour of your time, one hug, one act of service, or one little gift might point someone to Jesus.

notes

notes

sources

1. Chad Brand et al., eds., *Holman Illustrated Bible Dictionary* (Nashville, TN: Holman Reference, 2003), 1054.
2. Chelsea Stanley, "Daughters, God Has Made You Sons," February 15, 2018, https://www.desiringgod.org/articles/daughters-god-has-made-you-sons.
3. Gary Chapman, *The 5 Love Languages* (Chicago, IL: Moody Publishers, 2014).